American Indian Clothes

American Indian Clothes

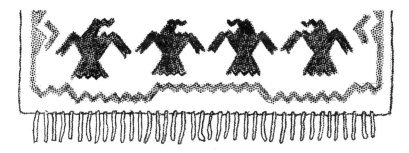

and How to Make Them

ALEX WHITNEY

Illustrated by Marie and Nils Ostberg

DAVID McKAY COMPANY, INC.
NEW YORK

Library of Congress Cataloging in Publication Data

Whitney, Alex.
  American Indian clothes and how to make them.

  Bibliography: p.
  Includes index.
  SUMMARY: Includes instructions for making and
adorning such articles as breeches, shirts, dresses,
belts, moccasins, headdresses, armbands, anklets,
jewelry, and pouches.
  1. Indian craft—Juvenile literature. 2. Indians
of North America—Costume and adornment—Juvenile
literature. 3. Costumes-Juvenile literature.
  [1. Indian craft. 2. Indians of North America—
Costume and adornment. 3. Costume. 4. Handicraft]
I. Ostberg, Marie. II. Ostberg, Nils. III. Title.
TT22.W48   646.4'7   78-20334
ISBN 0-679-20502-0

1 2 3 4 5 6 7 8 9 10

Manufactured in the United States of America

For Barbara Whitney and Jennifer Jones

Contents

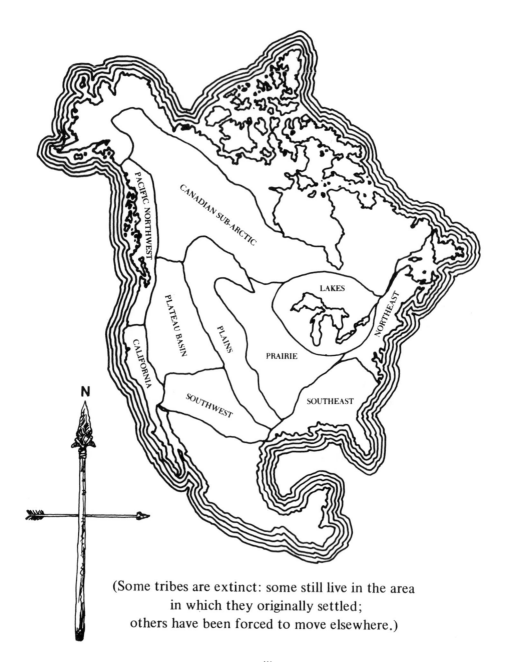

(Some tribes are extinct: some still live in the area
in which they originally settled;
others have been forced to move elsewhere.)

MAJOR INDIAN TRIBES OF THE NORTH AMERICAN CONTINENT

PACIFIC NORTHWEST

Bellabella
Bellacoola
Chinook
Haida
Klamath
Kwakiutl
Makah
Nootka
Quileute
Quinault
Salish
Tlinglit
Tsimshian

CALIFORNIA

Chumash
Costano
Hupa
Karok
Maidu
Mission
Miwok
Modoc
Pomo
Salinan
Shasta
Wintun
Yokuts
Yurok

SOUTHWEST

Acoma
Apache
Arizona Papago
Chiricahua Apache
Havasupai
Hopi
Maricopa
Navajo
Pima
Pueblo
Walapai
Yavapai
Yuma
Zuni

PLATEAU-BASIN

Bannock
Cayuse
Flathead
Gosiute
Kutenai
Mono
Nez Percé
Paiute
Panamint
Paviotso
Piegan
Shoshoni
Shuswap

Thompson
Ute
Washo
Yakima

Shawnee
Wichita
Yankton

LAKES

Chippewa
Fox
Kickapoo
Menomini
Ottawa
Pottawatomi
Sauk
Winnebago

PLAINS

Arapaho
Assinboin
Blackfoot
Cheyenne
Comanche
Crow
Gros Ventre
Kiowa
Oglala Sioux
Sioux
Teton Sioux

SOUTHEAST

Alabamu
Apalachee
Atakapa
Biloxi
Caddo
Calusa
Catawba
Cherokee
Chickahominy
Chickasaw
Chitimacha
Choctaw
Creek
Koasati
Natchez
Powhatan
Quapaw
Seminole
Timucua
Tuscarora

PRAIRIE

Arikara
Dakota
Hidatsa
Illinois
Ioway
Kansas
Mandan
Miami
Missouri
Omaha
Osage
Oto
Pawnee
Ponca
Santee

NORTHEAST

Abnaki
Algonqui
Beothuk
Conestoga
Delaware
Erie
Iroquois
Leni-Lenape
Mohican
Malecite
Massachuset
Micmac
Nanticoke
Narragansett
Passamaquoddy
Pennacook
Penobscot
Pequot
Powhaton
Shinnecock

CANADIAN SUB-ARCTIC

Algonkian
Beaver
Carrier
Chipewyan
Cree
Dogrib
Hare
Ingalik
Kaska
Khotana
Kutchin
Montagnais
Nahane
Naskapi
Sarsi
Satudene
Sekani
Slave
Tahaina
Yellow Knife

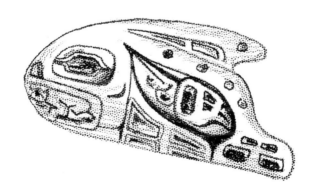

Foreword

There appears to be no limit to what Native Americans could do to make their clothes attractive, durable, and functional. This was due to their expertise in clothing construction, their sense of design and color, and the materials they obtained from natural sources—plants, mammals, birds, fish, shells, and metal, among them.

American Indian fashions varied from tribe to tribe, depending on the environment of the area in which each lived. Basically, however, their clothing was divided into three categories: everyday, ceremonial, and war apparel.

It's easy to understand why their attire has been admired and emulated throughout much of the world for many centuries. The fact that each year increasing numbers of people buy or copy Indian fashions proves the obvious: Native American clothes are timeless.

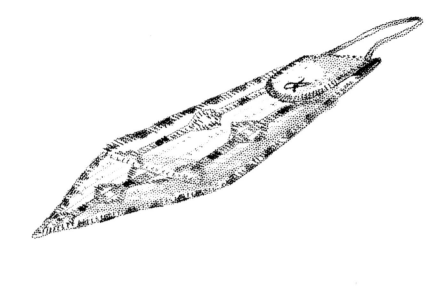

1

Skinwork and Fur

Buckskin was the most widely used clothing material of the Native American. Waterproof, windproof, and washable, it was made from the skin of the antelope, moose, elk, caribou, buffalo, or male deer. Deerskin, however, was considered to be the finest source of buckskin.

After an animal had been skinned, its hair and flesh were scraped from its hide. The hide was then plunged into a pot of boiling water to which had been added the animal's brains and liver. After soaking in this preparation for several days, the hide was pounded, kneaded, and stretched—a process that made it soft and white. While this partially treated skin was often fashioned into dresses for women and very young children, the skin became stiff when wet, so it was usually smoked, or tanned.

Rawhide was stretched on a drying frame made of saplings.

Tanning was done by suspending the hide on poles above a smoldering fire in a pit for several hours. This treatment resulted in a pliable skin that varied in color from light buff to dark tan. If corncobs were added to the fire, the hide turned yellow. Rusty-red shades were obtained by immersing the tanned skin in a solution of oak bark and water. The hide became scarlet when steeped in a mixture of peach bark or red cedar bark, wood ashes, and boiling water.

The preparation of buffalo buckskin differed from that of other animal hides. First, the meat and tissue clinging to the hide were removed with a chisel-like tool made of bone. Then, while the skin was drying in the sun, it was pounded with a heavy rock and planed with a horn tool to make the hide thinner and more supple. Finally, it was de-haired with a bone scraper. This process was almost always done by groups of women (reminiscent of our old-fashioned quilting

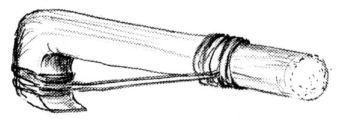
A bent antler tool was used to plane and thin hides.

bees), who then fashioned the treated buckskin into moccasin soles and winter clothing.

Rawhide, or untanned buckskin, was also made into moccasin soles as well as leggings, vests, and thongs. A hide was first stretched on a frame or on the ground. After all traces of flesh and tissue had been removed, the skin was placed in a running stream overnight or sprinkled with wood ashes and buried in the ground for several days to make the next step—the de-hairing process—easier to accomplish. The finished hide was tough, lightweight, and often translucent. If the hide was left untreated, it shrank and became very hard. When wet, it could be bent and even molded. Known as *shaganappi,* or iron leather, it was used for shields, drumheads, and ropes.

Many kinds of furs were used by Native Americans for their winter clothes and for decorations. The pelts ranged from those of large animals, such as bears, buffaloes, and caribou, to otters, beavers, rabbits, and other smaller species.

In many regions, strips of rabbit fur were braided or woven into soft outer garments. During the colder times of year, buffalo and bearskin robes were worn by both men

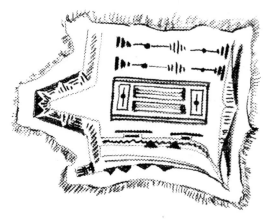

painted buffalo fur robe

3

and women. Almost all women and children in the sub-arctic and other northern zones wore fur mittens, fur-lined moccasins, and fur capelets.

Fur ceremonial costumes were worn throughout North America. For example, the California tribal costume for the White Deer Dance consisted of a headband made of wolf fur and a toga-like garment made of deer fur. Chippewa ceremonial leggings were fashioned from the fur of the black bear, while the Tlinglit and other Indians of the Pacific Northwest wore ermine or white weasel decorations on their ceremonial shirts and vests.

Fur hides were soaked in cold water to soften them and keep them from rotting. Then, a bone-fleshing tool, called a beam, was used to carefully remove the meat and fat from the underskin. Next, bear grease or other animal fat was lightly massaged into the fur to preserve it and to protect it from overly hot or dry conditions and harmful insects.

Both the skin and fur clothing of Native Americans were decorated with a wide variety of materials and dressings—some elaborate, some simple. More importantly, the American Indians' vast knowledge of preparing and treating hides and furs, combined with their patience and skill, has never been emulated by modern-day methods.

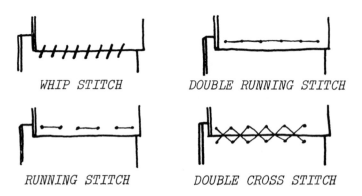

WHIP STITCH *DOUBLE RUNNING STITCH*

RUNNING STITCH *DOUBLE CROSS STITCH*

stitches used for sewing skin clothing

2

Weaving, Textiles, and Dyes

American Indians wove fine and coarse textiles with a wide range of materials, using three main techniques—finger weaving, plaiting, and netting. Loom weaving was practiced only by Southwestern tribes.

Materials for weaving the textiles stemmed from many sources: animal hair, fur strips, feathers, yucca fiber, hemp, nettles, grasses, cotton, milkweed, and the inner bark of cedar and basswood trees.

In the Southwest, before early Spanish explorers and settlers introduced the Indians to woolen cloth (which the Navajo unraveled and re-wove into their famous *bayeta* blankets), tribal women of the area wove textiles out of cotton or vegetal fibers on girdleback looms. The long

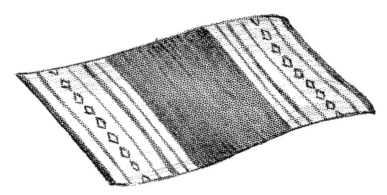

Navajo dresses were made of two pieces of
woven wool, such as this bordered rectangle.

threads (warp) were strung between two poles. The upper
pole was usually tied to a tree; the lower pole had an
attached belt which the weaver placed around her waist.
She was able to control the tension of the warp threads with
her own movements. The cross threads (weft) were woven
over and under the warp threads with the fingers or a small
stick.

In addition to weaving cotton textiles, southwestern and
southeastern Indians also made feather capes by tying
feathers to a base of fibers during the weaving process.

Outside the cotton-growing regions, finger weaving and
plaiting were the most commonly used techniques. In finger

double-band plaiting

netting

6

weaving, the warp threads were loosely suspended from a horizontal pole, supported by two uprights. No tools, other than the fingers, were used.

Netting was done by fastening the end of a strand of material to a needle-like bobbin and passing it back over itself to make loops. The loops were then knotted or twisted.

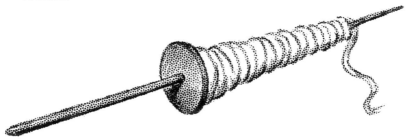

The spindle, a forerunner of the spinning wheel, was used to wind materials for textiles.

Cotton, animal hair, and fiber-weaving materials were prepared in several steps. First, they were cleaned and carded (cotton was fluffed by whipping). Next, the material was rolled on spindles and pulled into strands. In most cases, the finished threads were dyed, immersed in cold water to set the colors, then allowed to dry.

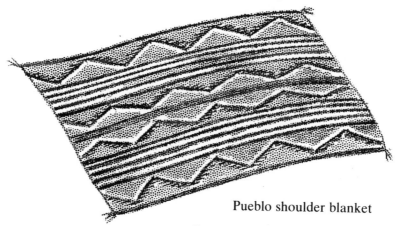

Pueblo shoulder blanket

Of all the natural textile dyes, yellow shades were the easiest to obtain. They were often made by boiling wild sage or sagebrush leaves and twigs with raw alum. Red and pink dyes were made with a mixture of red clay, rainwater, and hemlock bark. Sumac leaves and pine resin boiled in water produced brown shades; if pitch was added to the solution, the dye became dark blue or black.

Textile dyes were also made from stones, roots, nuts, and berries. Huckleberries were boiled with maidenhair ferns for purple shades. Green colors were made by steeping grasses or yucca fibers in boiling water.

The Native American possessed an outstanding sense of form and color. The textile shades and patterns, favored by each tribe, reflected the shapes and colors of the wildlife, water, soil, and plants of their surroundings.

3

Beadwork

Native American beads have often been mistakenly referred to as "wampum." Actually, wampum, or Indian "money," is a contraction of the Algonquin word *wankpumpeag,* meaning "a string of beads." The Algonquin and Iroquois introduced wampum—cylindrical beads made of the inner purple or white parts of clamshells—as a form of currency in their tradings with white settlers.

Although almost every tribe in North America made beads out of saltwater or freshwater shells, they also relied upon many other sources: fish and animal bones, pebbles, claws, nuts, seeds, quills, berries, horn, metals, clay, and semiprecious stones. Tribes of the Southwest specialized in turquoise and silver beads, while those living along the

pony beads

seed beads

wampum beads

Pacific coast used abalone shells and dried berries. Plains and Prairie tribes made beads from clay, nuts, and birds' claws; Southeastern Indians preferred soapstone and metals.

Native American beadwork techniques fall into four categories: netted, spot-stitch, lazy-stitch, and woven.

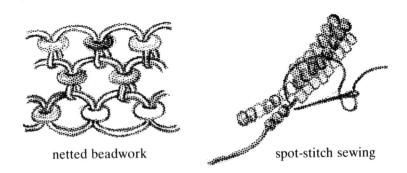

netted beadwork

spot-stitch sewing

lazy-stitch beadwork

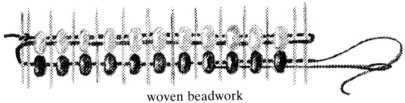

woven beadwork

Woven beadwork was done with a simple loom and a bone awl. In this single-weft method, beads were strung on sinew threads and plaited through the warps.

Spot-stitch beadwork was done by placing threaded beads in a design and sewing them in place—a technique popular with Northwestern and Plains Indians.

Lazy-stitch beadwork, characteristic of the Sioux, Fox, Ute, and Arapaho tribes, was done with two sewing awls and two sinew threads. The beads were strung on the sinews, then sewn to the surface of the material to be decorated.

Paiute beaded capelet

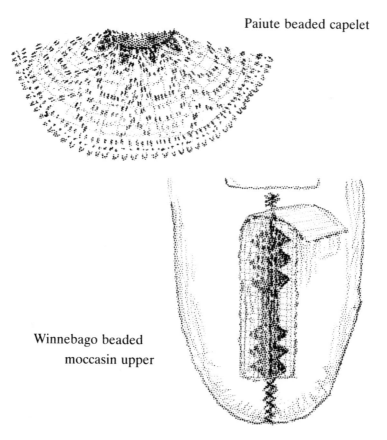

Winnebago beaded
moccasin upper

There were several ways of making netted beadwork, which was used to cover rounded surfaces, such as collars, capes, and medallions. The most widely used method consisted of stringing beads, a few at a time, on sinew thread, then sewing them to a garment in short, parallel rows. This tended to raise the beads between the stitches and give the effect of a ridged surface.

The beginning beadworker should start with simple designs such as those following. The patterns can be enlarged or reduced according to the size of the beads and the areas to be decorated.

You can enlarge or reduce these designs by drawing them to scale on graph paper, or you can create designs of your own.

4

Quillwork

The Oglala Sioux claimed that quillwork, an art unique to North American Indians, originated in a dream of one of their tribeswomen. She said that a supernatural woman had taught her how to use the tubular quills of the porcupine to decorate ceremonial costumes. However, almost every North American tribe decorated their clothing with quillwork.

Wrapping—a quillwork technique practiced by the Northeast and Pacific Northwest Indians—was done by folding quills around a single thread, which was then sewn in a pattern to the surface of a garment.

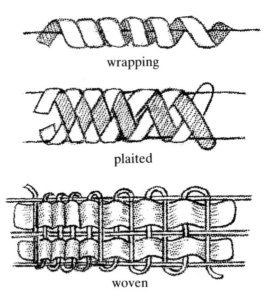

wrapping

plaited

woven

Plaited, or woven, quillwork was the most commonly used method, and it represents the finest example of the art. When a band of threads had been plaited on stretched fiber warps, the quills were woven in and out of the wefts.

Porcupine quills are hollow. Their length, thickness, and flexibility depend upon the parts of the animal from which they are plucked. The thinnest, most delicate quills are found on the porcupine's neck; coarser and larger quills come from its tail and back.

Porcupine quills are hollow.

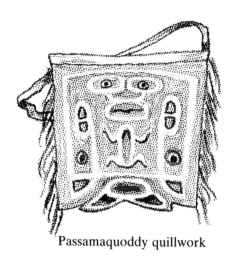

Passamaquoddy quillwork

When a porcupine had been killed and plucked, the women washed its quills and sorted them according to size. After they had been moistened by one of the quillworkers— who held the quills in her mouth because it was believed that saliva made them more pliable than water—the quills were flattened with a bone implement or drawn between the teeth. The final step in their preparation was boiling them in dyes made with water and flowers, vegetables, roots, or bark.

Flat, plastic cord, available in many craft and hobby shops and from the suppliers listed in the back of the book, makes an excellent substitute for real porcupine quills.

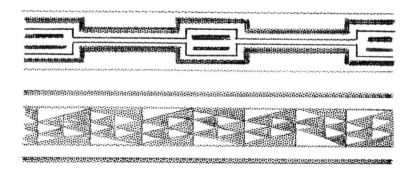

5

Featherwork

The feathers of wild turkeys, hawks, woodpeckers, owls, cardinals, condors, and many other birds were used to decorate the headgear and other apparel of the Native American. But the feathers of the eagle—both Golden and Bald—were prized above all others.

The Cherokee and other southeastern tribes, as an example, believed they were descended from the eagle—their symbol for courage and "dominion in flight." Only those warriors who had proved their bravery and skill on the battlefield were allowed to wear the eagle's feathers.

The most flamboyant featherwork was found in the headgear of the Plains and Plateau Indians. (See also the chapter on headdresses.) Their classic, long-tailed war bonnets consisted of matched eagle plumes in graduated sizes. Fluffs—the soft feathers growing near the tip of a bird's tail—were used as the base for the larger eagle plumes.

There were several ways in which Native Americans obtained eagle feathers. Sometimes, a brave squatted in a pit in the ground and concealed himself with a cover of brush, topped with chunks of rabbit or deer meat. An opening was left in the brush so that the brave could grab the tail feathers of an eagle when the bird swooped down to take the bait. Another method of accumulating eagle feathers was done by capturing the young birds while still in the nest. The eagles were then tethered and kept solely for their feathers.

The plumage of eagles, hawks, and egrets were used for "coup" feathers—comparable to the campaign ribbons and medals worn by our military. Notches or spots of paint on a feather, or the angle at which it was worn, designated the wearer's deeds of exceptional valor.

eagle feather and fluff

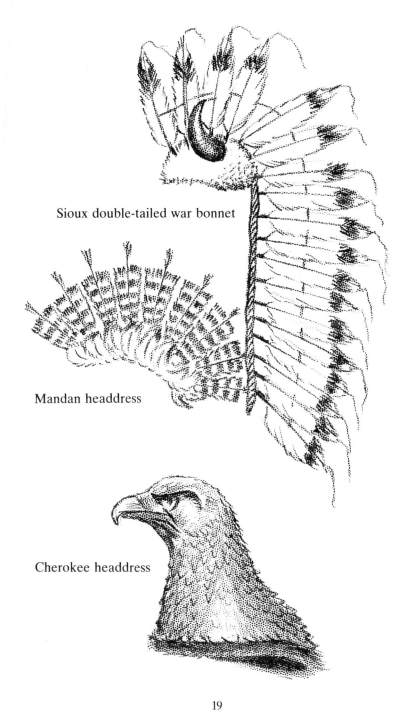

Sioux double-tailed war bonnet

Mandan headdress

Cherokee headdress

19

To prepare plucked feathers, the Indians lightly coated each one with animal grease or fish oil. This kept the feathers from drying out and from becoming dark or yellowed by smoke from cooking and council fires. Fluffs were soaked in cold water for two days, then patted gently with the fingers until all dirt and stains had been removed.

Because eagles, hawks, and other species are on the endangered list, chicken or turkey feathers (plain, dyed, or painted) can be used for the projects described in the chapter on headdresses. Imitation eagle feathers and fluffs are also available from suppliers listed at the back of the book.

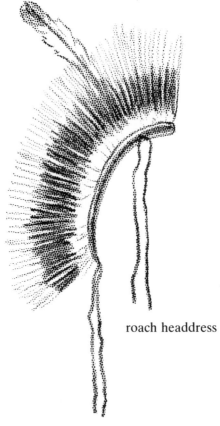

roach headdress

6

Shellwork, Bonework, and Horn Craft

Many kinds of Native American jewelry and shell-embroidered attire have been unearthed by archaeologists. Shells were also important items in intertribal trade; and in the eighteenth and nineteenth centuries, fur merchants even imported shells for trade with the Indians.

For their ornaments and decorations, almost every tribe used snail, cowrie, mussel, scallop, conch, whelk, and clam shells. A string of clam-shell beads was made by first grinding away the shells' rough exteriors with a stone scraper. Next, the shells were shaped with a knife, and holes were drilled in their centers. They were then polished and strung on vegetal fibers, sinew thread, or rawhide thongs.

Southwestern tribes, particularly the Pueblo, Hopi, and Zuni, carved exquisite pendants and inlaid their rings and bracelets with the centers of clamshells, obtained through

clamshell beads

trade with California Indians. Chinook pendants and beads were made from the iridescent interiors of abalone shells, while the spiral centers of conches were fashioned into hair and ear ornaments by southeastern Indians.

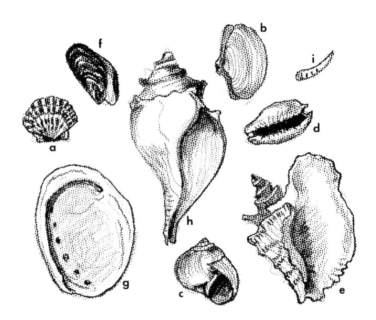

a. scallop *b.* clam *c.* snail *d.* cowrie *e.* conch
f. mussel *g.* abalone *h.* whelk *i.* dentalium

Shell embroidery was popular with every North American tribe. It was done by stringing small shells (usually snail) together and sewing them to skins or textiles. A well-known example of this art is "Powhatan's Mantle," a shell-

Powhatan's shell-embroidered mantle

embroidered buckskin cape that once belonged to the Algonquin chief, and that is now in a museum in England.

Another form of shell embroidery, practiced by Indians in the Northwest, was done with dentalia—long, cone-shaped shells found along the Pacific coast.

Native Americans made use of another natural resource for their ornamentation. Bone was made into a variety of items, such as earrings, necklaces, bracelets, and combs. Most of the items were made from the vertebrae of birds, rabbits, raccoons, and deer.

Some of the most familiar forms of this craft were the hair-pipe breastplates and long necklaces of the Plains

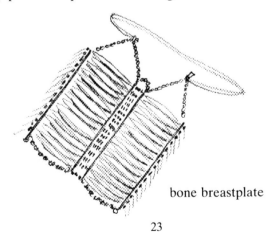

bone breastplate

23

carved antler comb

Indians. The bones were scraped and cleaned, and placed in the sun to bleach. They were then carved or engraved with a sharp-pointed awl.

Horn was also widely used by the Indians because it was easily worked when heated. Two pieces of horn, for instance, could be welded by boiling the pieces in water and pressing them firmly together. The horns of buffalo, deer, elk, and mountain sheep were shaped into many kinds of articles, such as spoons, bowls, and jewelry. Clothing decorations were frequently made by heating horn and setting it in a wooden or stone mold. The horn was then engraved, carved, or inlaid with shell.

The Mandan and other Prairie tribes made jewelry out of deer antlers by soaking the horn in water and bending it into shape to form bracelets. Tribes of the Northeast made deer-antler hair ornaments. The best-known are those of the Iroquois, who carved tiny figurines and symbols on their combs.

7

Sewing Equipment

Knives—fashioned out of stone, shell, hardwood, and even animals' teeth—were used by Native Americans to cut out the pieces for their garments.

The thick, hard bones of the bison, elk, caribou, deer, and bear provided the Indians with excellent material for making awls and needles. Sandstone was used to smooth

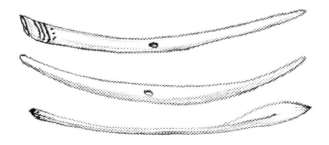

bone needles and pins

the rough edges of the implements, most of which were pointed at both ends. Awls were used to puncture holes in hides through which thongs or sinew threads were passed.

Animal sinew was the source of the Indians' thread, and was used to stitch a wide variety of materials. It was made from the large tendons along the backbones of the buffalo or deer. When the tendons—usually about two feet long—had been thoroughly dried in the sun and pounded until soft, they were shredded into filaments of various thicknesses.

Mandan bone knife

Glue was often used for sealing and reinforcing the seams of winter robes and moccasins and for attaching feathers to headdresses. One kind of glue was made from the neck muscles of the buffalo or elk. The muscles were boiled in water for several days to make a jelly-like substance.

Northeastern tribes made glue by boiling deer sinew and antlers in water, while California Indians made their glue from the gum resin of mesquite trees and the roots of the soap plant.

Perhaps the strongest and most durable glue was made by the Cherokee. Called *bigui,* its base was pitch extracted from evergreen trees. The pitch was boiled until it became pure resin, then it was mixed with wood ashes.

Cherokee copper knife with antler handle

8

Headdresses

A Native American headdress was once a method of tribal identification because each tribe had its own type of headgear. In fact, each feather of a headdress usually had a special meaning. For instance, if the tip of a plume was cut off, it meant that the wearer's enemy had been killed. A split feather denoted that the wearer had been wounded in battle. If a warrior's roach was dyed scarlet, it showed he had been the first to wound or kill an enemy in battle.

Perhaps the most familiar and dramatic headdress of all Native American cultures was the large, feathered war bonnet of the Sioux and the Apache. Each bonnet consisted of matched eagle feathers, attached to a cap with a decorated band in the front and strips of ermine at the

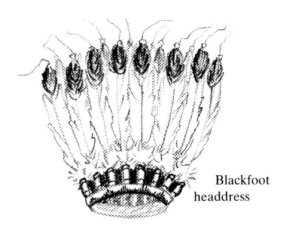

Blackfoot
headdress

sides. Most of the war bonnets had long single or double tails.

Braves of many tribes, particularly the Cheyenne, wore a single, upright eagle feather inserted in a headband. Other warriors often sported roaches, made of animal hair, and woven in such a way that the hair stood straight up. A feather, rising from the roach's forward center, was held in place by drawing a lock of the warrior's hair through a hole in the roach's front end and tying it in a knot.

The different types of Indian headdresses were endless. California tribes adorned theirs with numerous small feathers, arranged in mosaic-like patterns; the Mohican, Abnaki, and Algonkian wore bright red headdresses, made by sewing woodpecker scalps to dyed deerskin strips. In the Southeast, shamans and chieftains often wore stuffed owls—their symbols for wisdom—as headgear.

Pawnee fur hat

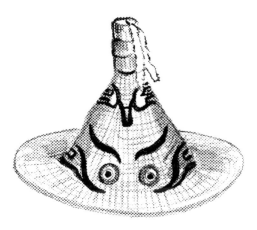

Painted Tlinglit ceremonial hats were woven of spruce roots and cedar strips.

Needless to say, the kind of war bonnet and headdress belonging to each tribe depended upon the area in which the tribe lived. Caps, turbans, and roaches were more suited to heavily wooded terrains than the elaborate, feathered headgear of the tribes who lived in the plains, prairies, and desert regions. In winter, Northeast, Northwest, sub-arctic and Lakes Indians usually wore fur turbans, made of otter, badger, or beaver pelts. The Iroquois preferred *gustowehs,* fur-and-leather turbans adorned with several plumes.

PAWNEE HEADPIECE

Materials
approximately 1 square yard of light-colored felt
crown of an old felt hat
2 feathers
tape measure
pair of scissors
needle and heavy-duty thread
sharp knife or razor
waterproof felt-tipped markers

Fig. 1

1. With a knife or a razor, cut two slits in one side of the hat crown, as shown in Fig. 1.

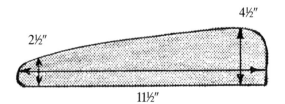

Fig. 2

2. Fold the yard of felt in half, and cut two pieces (A and B), according to Fig. 2.

Fig. 3

3. Cut two circles (medallions) of felt, each 2½″ in diameter. Decorate them with felt-tipped markers, as shown in Fig. 3.

4. Sew each circle to each side of the headpiece, as shown in Fig. 4.

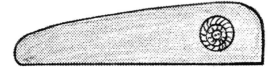

Fig. 4

5. Sew piece A to the hat crown, as shown in Fig. 5. Sew piece B to the other side of the crown, making sure that the tapered end of the felt piece, B, is even with the end of piece A.

Fig. 5

6. Sew the ends of the felt pieces, A and B, as shown in Fig. 6.

Fig. 6

Fig. 7

7. Insert the two feathers in the slits, as shown in Fig. 7.

Note: The medallions can be decorated with beadwork instead of the waterproof markers. See chapter on beadwork for stitches and designs.

CROW HEADDRESS

Materials

crown of an old felt hat
30-40 feathers
2 bands of felt or leather, each 1½″ wide and ½″
    longer than the widest circumference of the
    hat crown
sharp knife or razor
tape measure
white glue or needle and heavy-duty thread
waterproof felt-tipped markers or acrylic paints
    and brush
pencil

1. With a knife or razor, cut evenly spaced ¼" slots (according to the number of feathers to be used) in the hat crown, as shown in Fig. 1.

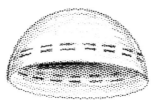

Fig. 1

2. Insert feathers in slots, and glue in place or sew to the hat crown, according to Fig. 2.

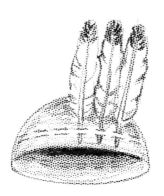

Fig. 2

3. With a pencil, draw designs on the felt or leather bands, as shown in Fig. 3. Color the designs.

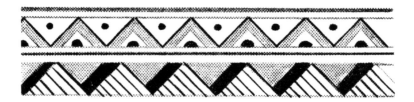

Fig. 3

4. Glue or sew two bands over the ends of the feathers, as shown in Fig. 4.

Fig. 4

9

Dresses and Capelets

For many people, the fringed and beaded buckskin garments of the Plains tribes typify Native American dresses.
Indian dresses, however, encompassed a variety of attractive and practical styles, and children's dresses were minia-
ture versions of them.

The basic dress design of the Pueblo and other southwestern tribes consisted of a *manta,* a woven cotton
rectangle, folded under the left arm and fastened over the
right shoulder. The basic Navajo dress was two-piece: an
ankle-length cotton skirt, and a shirt, usually decorated with
round, silver ornaments.

The brightly colored, cotton skirts and capelets of the
Seminole women were—and still are—among the most

decorative of all American Indian garments. Seminole women also wore countless strings of shell beads that covered their necks up to their chins.

Most of the tribeswomen, who lived in less temperate regions than the Southeast and Southwest, made their dresses out of two deerskins or similar hides, sewn together with sinew. The styles of the garments followed the shapes of the skins and hung loose from the shoulders.

Indian women in the Northeast usually fringed the hems and sleeves of their skin dresses, while Dakota tribeswomen preferred to trim their dresses with strips of white weasel fur. Women of the Crow, Sioux, and Blackfoot tribes decorated their skin garments with cowrie shells, beads, or quillwork.

Cheyenne dress, decorated with cowrie shells

Sioux dress and capelet   Pueblo women's
ceremonial costume

With the exception of the tribes living in warm regions
and in the sub-arctic zones, many women wore soft buckskin jumpers and separate sleeves, yokes, or capelets.
Apache tribeswomen changed their jumpers into ceremonial costumes by adding capelets painted with symbolic

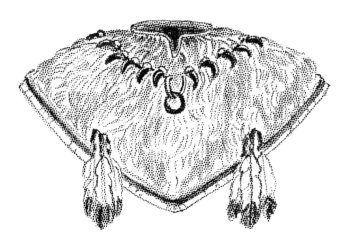

Chippewa bearskin cape, adorned with bear claws and feathers

designs. Indian women in the Pacific Northwest topped their jumpers with bearskin capelets, decorated with shells or bear claws.

In addition to donning skin dresses, Chippewa, Fox, Winnebago, and Menomoni tribeswomen wore dresses made of materials woven with threads made of the inner bark of basswood or cedar, milkwood fibers, and buffalo hair.

PLAINS INDIAN DRESS

Materials

buckskin, imitation suede, or almost any kind of
   plain fabric
pair of scissors
tape measure
waterproof marking pens in assorted colors or
   beadwork equipment needle and heavy-duty
   thread
paper for pattern
sewing machine (optional)
Note: See stitches for skinwork in chapter on skinwork.

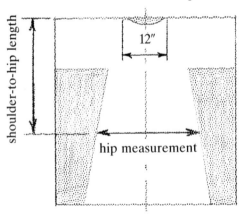

Fig. 1

1. Measure from the shoulder to the calf. Your fabric should be double this length. In order to make sure that the dress will hang loosely, measure around the hips and add four inches. Make a paper pattern, as shown in Fig. 1.

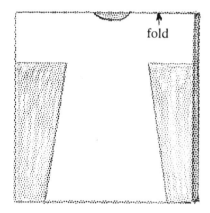

fold

Fig. 2

2. Fold the material according to Fig. 2, and cut out the dress, making sure that both sides are even. Sew along the lines indicated in Fig. 3.

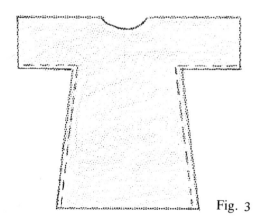

Fig. 3

3. If you wish, you can fringe the sleeves and hem of the dress. With waterproof marking pens, decorate the front and sleeves of the dress. Copy the Blackfoot, Sioux, and other designs shown in Fig. 4. Or, decorate the dress with beadwork. See chapter on beadwork for stitches and designs.

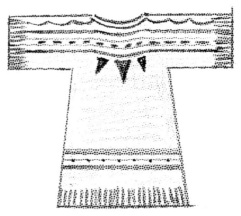

NAVAJO TWO-PIECE DRESS

Materials for the skirt
solid-colored cotton fabric
pair of scissors
tape measure
needle and thread
sewing machine (optional)
string
banding or braid
snaps or hooks-and-eyes

1. Measure waistline and add 2" for lap-over where the skirt and waistband will be fastened.

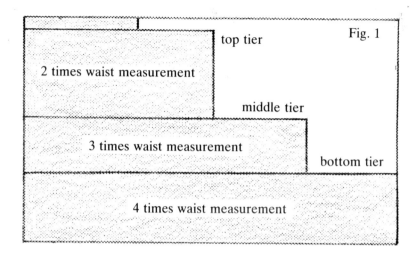

Fig. 1

top tier

2 times waist measurement

middle tier

3 times waist measurement

bottom tier

4 times waist measurement

2. For the waistband, cut a strip of the skirt fabric 4″ wide and as long as the waist measurement. Measure from the waist to the ankle and divide the fabric by three to make the three tiers of the skirt, according to Fig. 1. Gather and sew one tier to the waistband. Then gather and sew the second tier to the first tier and the bottom tier to the middle section. Then fold the skirt in half, and sew from the bottom to 7″ from the waistband.

1″ in

3. Sew banding or braid over the seams of the tiers and around the bottom of the skirt, as shown in Fig. 2. Sew on waistband fasteners.

Fig. 2

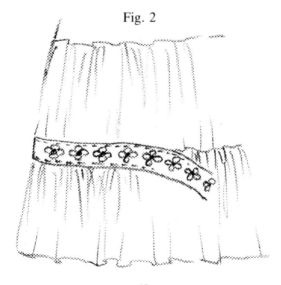

4. In order for the skirt to have an authentic Navajo appearance, thoroughly rinse it in warm water, but do not wring it out. While it is dripping wet, hold the skirt by the waistband and fold, as shown in Fig. 3.

Fig. 3

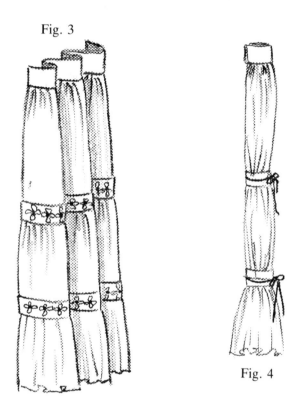

Fig. 4

5. Tie two pieces of string around the skirt where the seams are, as shown in Fig. 4. Hang up the skirt to dry.

Note: Only cotton fabric must be used for the skirt; drip-dry materials will not achieve the pleated and vertically wrinkled look of the real Navajo skirt.

NAVAJO BLOUSE

Navajo women originally wore simple, two-piece dresses of cotton and, sometimes, of skins. But since the 1870s, their blouses have been made of velvet. You can make a blouse to wear with the Navajo skirt by following the intructions given on a blouse pattern similar to the one shown in Fig. 6. It can be made of velvet, flannel, synthetic leather, wool, or heavy cotton. Or you can buy a collarless, long-sleeved blouse and give it a "Navajo look" by adding several silvery buttons on the front and sleeves, as shown in Fig. 7. This costume should be worn with a leather belt, buckled or decorated in silver.

SEMINOLE INDIAN TWO-PIECE DRESS

Materials
plain cotton or drip-dry fabric
pair of scissors
tape measure
needle and thread
sewing machine (optional)
braid
rickrack (assorted colors)
¾" elastic

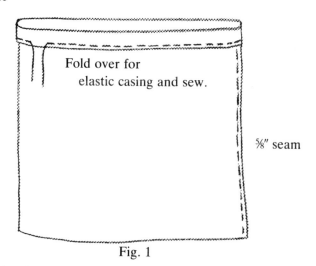

Fold over for
elastic casing and sew.

⅝" seam

Fig. 1

1. For the skirt, measure the length from the waistline
    to just above the ankle. Add 3" to the measure-
    ment of the hips and cut the material in a rectangle.
    The length should be the measurement from the
    waist to hem; and the width should be the hip
    measurement plus 3". Fold the fabric in half and
    sew the side seam. Hem one side of the rectangle
    and put an elastic band through the casing for the
    waistline, as shown in Fig. 1. Sew on strips of

rickrack and braid around the skirt, as shown in Fig. 2. Hem the skirt.

Fig. 2

2. To make the capelet, or the top of the dress, measure from the neck to the wrist and cut the material in a rectangle. Gather the material on a wide neckband, as shown in Fig. 3. Sew braid borders around the bottom of the capelet. The capelet is pulled over the head.

material

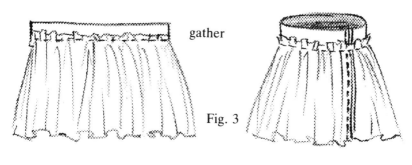

gather

Fig. 3

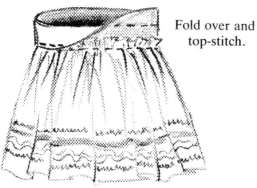

Fold over and
top-stitch.

Note: The true Seminole dress is a colorful patchwork design incorporating many pieces of multicolored cottons, sewn together. The top of the dress can be in a color that contrasts with the skirt. A simple white blouse would be suitable to wear under the capelet.

LAKES INDIAN CAPELET

Materials

1 square yard of buckskin, synthetic leather, or
  felt
pair of scissors
needle and heavy-duty thread
waterproof marking pens in assorted colors or
  beadwork equipment

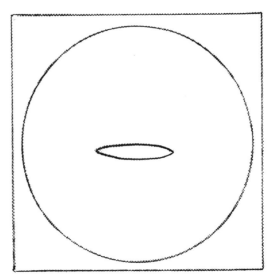

Fig. 1

1. Make a paper pattern, according to Fig. 1. Be sure the neck opening is large enough to slip easily over the head. The width of the capelet should extend no more than 1″ beyond the shoulder.

2. Fringe the capelet all the way around, as shown in Fig. 2.

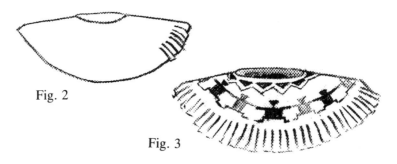

Fig. 2

Fig. 3

3. Decorate the capelet with designs, such as those shown in Fig. 3. Color the designs with waterproof markers or decorate with beadwork. See stitches and designs in chapter on beadwork.

48

10

Shirts

Indian men originally wore the same type of loose-fitting
shirt—a garment often mistakenly called a "war shirt."
Actually, it was a ceremonial shirt, worn by braves after
they returned from battle or by chiefs, shamans, and other
people of tribal authority. However, the shirts were seldom
worn for ceremonial dancing, because they were too hot.

Native American shirts were usually decorated with
fringe, beadwork, quillwork, paint, dye, shellwork, feathers, bonework, fur, or horn. The Dakota and the Cheyenne
trimmed their shirts with animal hair, and the tribes's
enemies called the garments "scalp shirts" because they
believed that the ornaments were made of human scalp
locks.

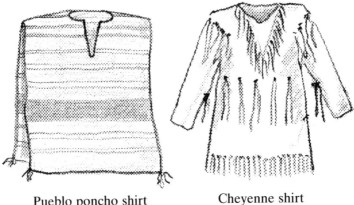

Pueblo poncho shirt   Cheyenne shirt

Some shirts, such as those of the Plains Indians, were elaborately ornamented with beaded symbols, while the Apache and other tribes of the Southwest preferred poncho-style shirts with painted designs.

Seminole patchwork shirt

With the exception of sub-arctic Indians and those who lived in extreme northern regions, Indian men usually wore vests instead of shirts, or were naked to the waist most of the year.

CHEROKEE SHIRT

Materials

buckskin or synthetic leather
glover's needle and heavy-duty thread
pair of scissors
pencil
tape measure
paper for pattern
beadwork equipment or waterproof, felt-tipped
    markers (optional)

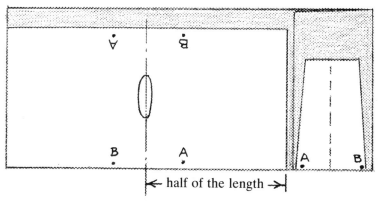

Mark center of shoulder and sleeves ⅝″ in from edge.
Fig. 1

1. This shirt should be fingertip length. Measure one
    of your own shirts, but cut out a paper pattern
    about 2″ wider, because the shirt should fit loosely.
    Place the pattern on the material, as shown in Fig.
    1. The pieces can be decorated with beadwork or
    waterproof, felt-tipped markers before they are
    sewn.

51

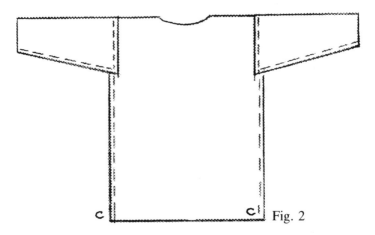
Fig. 2

2. Place point A on sleeve, over point A on shirt, matching the centers. Pin the sleeve to the shirt. Sew the sleeve from point A to point B. Then sew along the bottom of the sleeves and down the side of the shirt, from the armpit to point C, as shown in Fig. 2. Repeat this step on the other sleeve and side of the shirt.

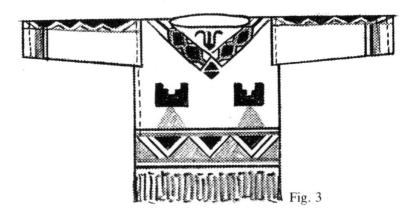
Fig. 3

3. Hem the cuff edges and the neck opening, and cut the fringe along the bottom of the shirt, as shown in Fig. 3. If you wish, you can paint the fringe red.

11

Vests

Until the early 1930s, many historians believed that the Indian vest was adopted from the Spanish explorers. But pieces of clothing, unearthed at mound sites in the Southeast and Northwest, indicate that Native Americans made vests long before Columbus sailed on his historic voyage.

Worn as decorative attire and as windbreakers, most vests were made of buckskin, but some were fashioned with the fur pelts of rabbit, muskrat, otter, and other animals. All vests were worn with or without shirts, depending on the climate and the time of year.

The Sioux favored solidly beaded, buckskin vests—works of art highly prized by early white settlers. Tribes in the Northeast and Lakes regions decorated their vests with quillwork or paint, while the Nootka and Chinook of the Pacific Northwest embroidered vests with dentalia— slender, cone-shaped shells, open at each end.

Nez Percé vest

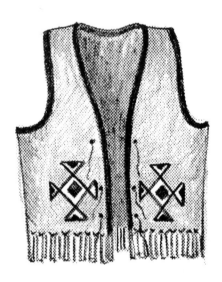

Choctaw vest

PAIUTE VEST

Materials
buckskin, felt, or synthetic leather
leather thong
glover's needle and heavy-duty thread
paper for pattern
pencil
tape measure
decorating materials (see step 4)

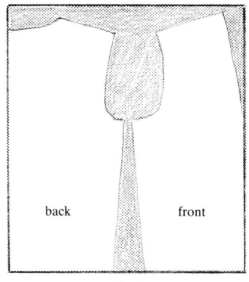

back   front

Fig. 1

1. The easiest way to make a vest is to make a paper pattern from a vest of your own. Place the vest on paper and draw an outline around it, according to Fig. 1. Be sure to add 1 or 2 inches to the side seams, because the vest should hang loosely.

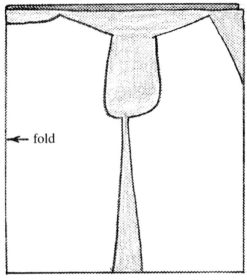

fold

Fig. 2

2. Cut out the back and two front sides of the vest, according to Fig. 2.

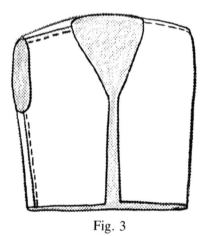

Fig. 3

3. Sew the shoulders and sides together, according to Fig. 3.

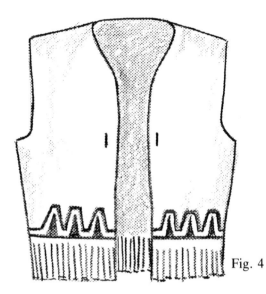

Fig. 4

4. Cut a slit in each of the front pieces of the vest for the thong ties. The bottom of the vest can be fringed or bound with braid, or you can decorate the front and back with beadwork, quillwork, paint, or colored felt-tipped markers, as shown in Figs. 4, 5, 6, and 7.

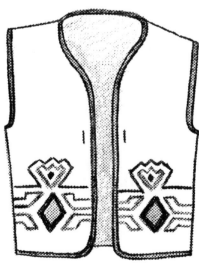

Fig. 5

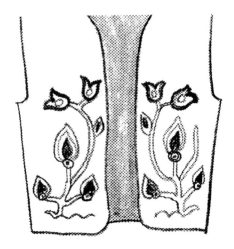

Fig. 6

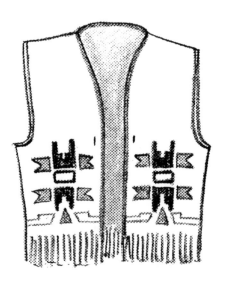

Fig. 7

12

Armbands and Anklets

Many of the men of almost every North American tribe wore armbands above the elbow, on the bare arm, or over a shirt sleeve. In winter, northern tribesmen wore their ornamental bands below the knee, over deerskin leggings.

The shaman (medicine man), chieftan, and other people of importance in a tribe often wore buckskin armbands with attached medallions designating their rank. Each medallion design was unique. No pattern was ever repeated exactly, and the colors and designs always varied.

Metalworkers of the Creek tribes made copper armbands embossed with symbolic designs, while the Hopi, Zuni, and Navajo fashioned armbands of engraved silver, set with pieces of turquoise. (See chapter on jewelry.) But most armbands were made of firm buckskin or rawhide and decorated with paint or beadwork.

Anklets, usually worn by men during ceremonial dances,

Kutenai anklet made of mountain goat hair

were made of buckskin strips adorned with painted designs, bells, shells, or fringes of animal hair.

Armbands and anklets never completely encircled the wearers' arms or ankles because they were tied on with leather strips or thongs to prevent them from slipping down.

60

CADDO MEDALLION ARMBAND

Materials

firm rawhide or synthetic leather
tape measure
pair of scissors
pencil
awl
felt-tipped markers (assorted colors)
ruler
leather thong, 6″ long
2–4 beads

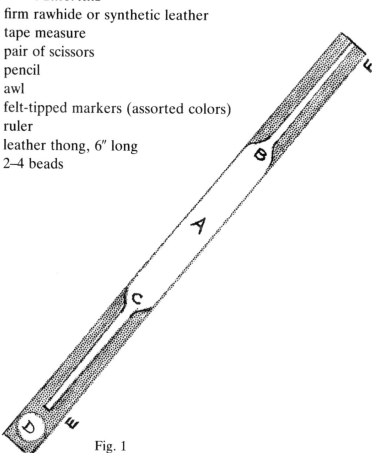

Fig. 1

1. Measure the circumference of the arm between the elbow and the shoulder. Draw and cut a pattern, according to Fig. 1. The length between points B and C should measure 2″ less than the circumference of the arm. The tying strips, E and F, should be no wider than ½″.

61

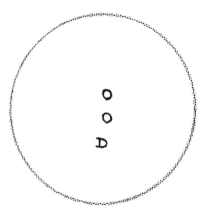

Fig. 2

2. Draw and cut piece D. With an awl or other pointed tool, make two holes for the thong, each ¼″ apart, in the exact centers of pieces A and D, as shown in Fig. 2.

Fig. 3

3. With a pencil, draw a design on piece D and color it with felt-tipped markers, as shown in Fig. 3.

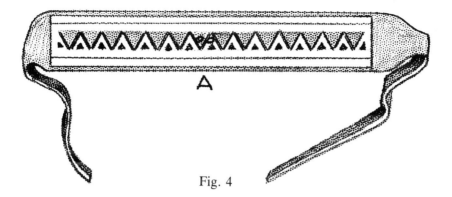

Fig. 4

4. Place piece D over piece A, matching the center holes in each piece. Pull the thong through the holes and knot on the outside of piece D, as shown in Fig. 4. Slip one or two beads on the end of each thong before knotting the ends, as shown in Fig. 5.

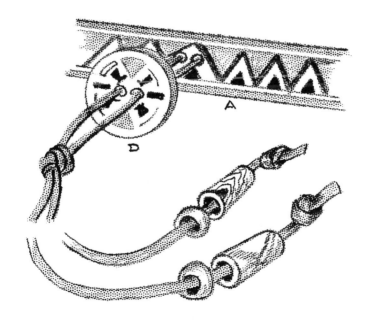

Fig. 5

63

SIOUX JINGLER ANKLET

Materials
firm buckskin, rawhide, or synthetic leather, 1¾"
   x 8"
leather thong, 36" long
6 small jingle bells with shanks
sharp penknife
pencil
ruler
pair of scissors

Fig. 1

1. Measure and mark seven spaces on the rawhide, as shown in Fig. 1.

2. Slit the rawhide with a knife at the points indicated in Fig. 2.

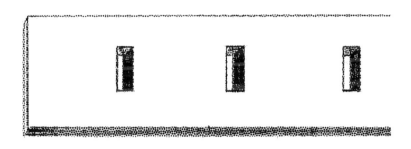

Fig. 2

3. Insert the shanks of the bells through the slits in the rawhide, as shown in Fig. 3.

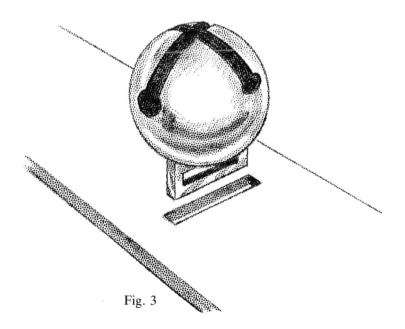

Fig. 3

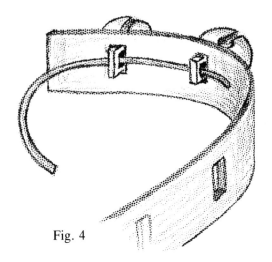

Fig. 4

4. Slip the leather thong through the shank of each
   bell, as shown in Fig. 4.

Note: The length of the piece of rawhide or synthetic leather
can be shortened or lengthened, according to the circumference measurement of the wearer's ankle.

13

Jewelry

The ingenuity and creativeness of Native Americans were, and still are, reflected in their jewelry—particularly in the magnificent turquoise-and-silver necklaces, rings, and bracelets of the Zuni, Hopi, and Navajo.

Copper, however, was the most commonly used metal; copper wire was twisted into bracelets and collars by the people of the Pacific Northwest, the Plains, Prairie, Plateau, and the Northeast.

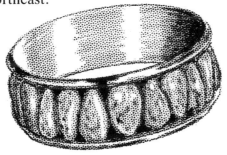

Hopi turquoise-and-silver bracelet

Zuni silver squash blossom necklace

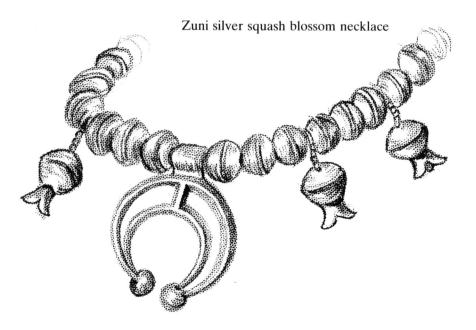

In addition to silver and copper, Indian jewelry was made with natural stones, seeds, bones, horns, shells, and a wide variety of other materials. Tribes throughout North America made bone-and-bead breastplates for protection and for ornaments, as well as bear-claw necklaces. Shell necklaces and pendants were especially popular in the coastal regions; tribes of the Vancouver area re-created the wildlife of their environment in their carved bone jewelry inlaid with shell.

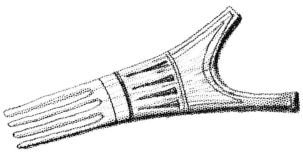

Iroquois carved antler comb

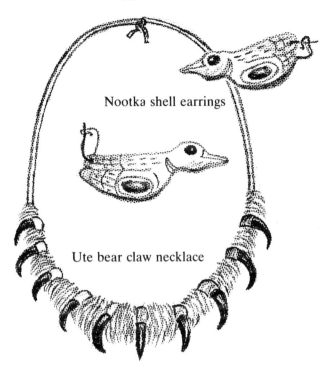

Nootka shell earrings

Ute bear claw necklace

SALISH OWL PENDANT

Materials

scallop shell
2 flat beads or metal buttons
1 flat, diamond-shaped bead or a diamond-
   shaped piece of sheet copper
wax marking pencil
drill and bit
white glue
cord, leather thong, or chain

Fig. 1

1. Using Fig. 1 as a guide, mark where the owl's eyes and beak will be. Carefully drill the hole for the cord, making sure the hole is big enough to insert the cord or thong.

2. Glue the bead eyes and beak in place, and allow the glue to dry thoroughly.

70

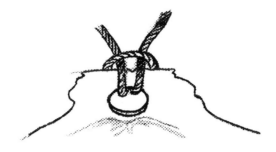

3. String the pendant on a cord, leather thong, or chain.

SHOSHONE NECKLACE

Materials

16 beads, ³⁄₁₆″ in diameter, and approximately 1″
   long
84 beads, ³⁄₁₆″ in diameter, and approximately ³⁄₁₆″
   long
1 two-hole shell button, 1½″ in diameter
2 cords or leather thongs, each 22″ long
2 cords or leather thongs, each 8″ long
1 cord or leather thong, 6″ long
3 leather separators, each ½″ x 1″
awl or hole puncher
large-eyed needle
pair of scissors

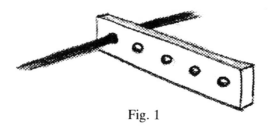

Fig. 1

1. Punch five holes in each leather separator. Insert one thong in the needle and into the top hole of a separator. Pull the thong through the hole, but leave several inches at one end for tying, as shown in Fig. 1.

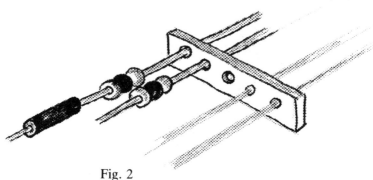

Fig. 2

2. String three of the ³⁄₁₆″ beads, one 1″ bead, and one leather separator. Repeat this sequence. Place the needle in the second hole of the last separator, and string a second row of beads, as shown in Fig. 2. When you come to the end of the row, tie the ends of the thong together.

3. String two more rows of beads and separators in the same way, leaving the center hole of each leather separator open.

4. Tie a knot at one end of each of the 8″ leather thongs. Insert one thong in the open center of each separator so that the knot is on the inside, as shown in Fig. 3.

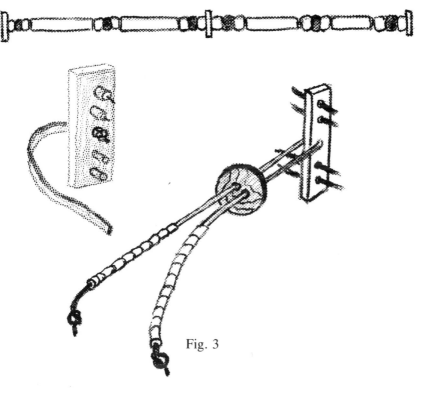

Fig. 3

5. Thread the 6″ leather thong through the center hole of the center leather separator, making sure that the ends of the thong are even. Pull one end through each hole of the 1½″ shell button, and

73

string each end with ten ³⁄₁₆″ beads. Tie a knot in each thong and trim the ends, as shown in Fig. 4.

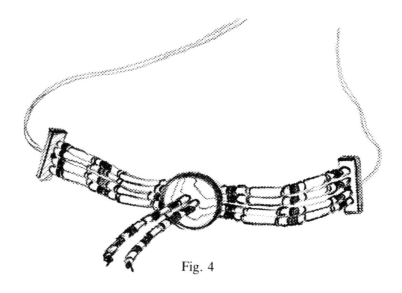

Fig. 4

Note: If you use beads of two or more colors, you can copy the design shown in Fig. 4 or create a pattern of your own. Leather separators are available from suppliers listed at the back of the book. You can also make your own separators out of rawhide or strap leather.

14

Belts and Sashes

Using a variety of materials at hand, Native Americans fashioned belts out of animal hair, hides, vegetal fibers, shells, bone, metal, and other natural substances. The belts

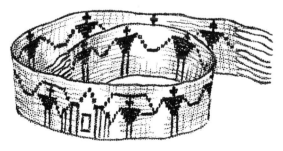

Algonkian beaded belt

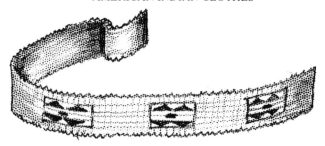

Arapaho belt, ornamented with quillwork

were usually worn for practical, rather than ornamental purposes. Carrying cases, small weapons, and tools were tucked under the belts or attached to them by leather

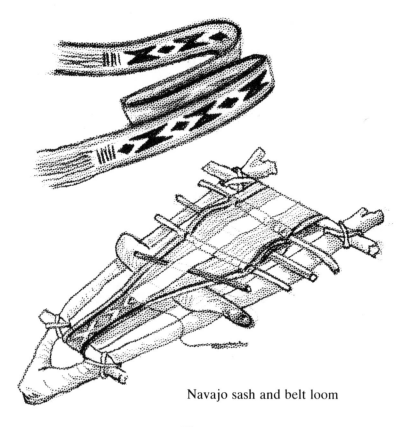

Navajo sash and belt loom

thongs. Woven belts and sashes often alternated as head-bands; and some tribes, such as the Iroquois, wore "trading" belts made of wampum (shell money).

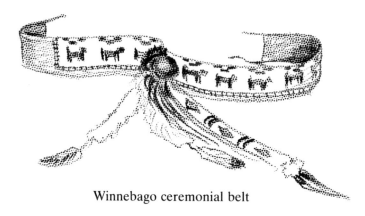

Winnebago ceremonial belt

Many of the Northwest Indians made belts out of twined cornhusks and plant fibers, while tribes of the Lakes area wore finger-woven belts and sashes. Although the life-styles of the Cherokee and the Pueblo were markedly different, both tribes made belts adorned with embossed metal. The braided belts of the Plains Indians were made from the neck hair of buffalo, and had a small loop at one end through which the other end was pulled to form a noose.

Beaded belts were popular with almost all tribes. Indians of the Pacific Northwest made belts of intricately designed beadwork, as did the Lenni-Lenape, whose beaded designs represented their victories in battle and treaties with neighboring tribes.

The Indians originally fashioned beads from seeds, stones, and the inner parts of clam, periwinkle, and other shells. (See chapters on beadwork and shells.) But with the arrival of the first Europeans came the Indians' introduction to glass beads. From the late 1700s on, the tribes preferred glass beadwork for decorating belts and other apparel.

FINGER-WOVEN CHIPPEWA TIE SASH

Materials
two 70-yard skeins of rug yarn, one rust or tan
  (A); one black or white (B)
pair of scissors
tape measure
pencil
dowel, 6″ long
hook

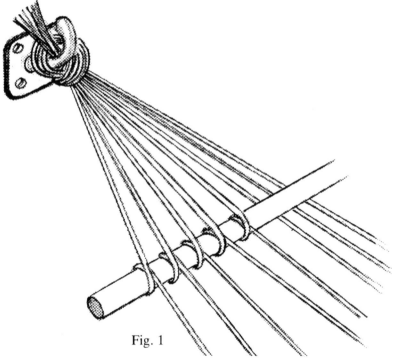

Fig. 1

Note: Only 8 strands are shown. You will have 16 strands.

1. Cut six 2-yard strands of color A and ten 2-yard
    strands of color B. Gather all strands into a bundle
    and tie at one end to a fixed hook. Wrap each

strand over, under, then over the dowel in the following color order: AAA BAB AAAA BB AA BB, as shown in Fig. 1.

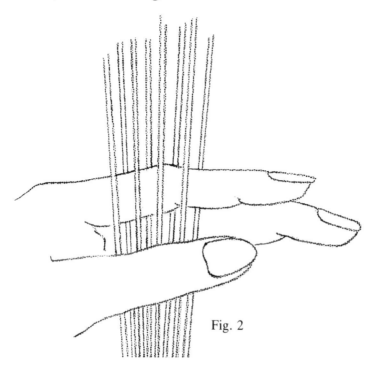

Fig. 2

2. Separate the odd-numbered strands from the even-numbered strands by holding the yarn bundle with the left hand and inserting the forefinger of the right hand from right to left over strand 1, under strand 2, over strand 3, and under strand 4. Continue this process between all strands; strand 16 will then be in the up position. This is called a "shed." Transfer the shed to the left hand, as shown in Fig. 2. The middle finger of the left hand should be under all the strands, and the forefinger should be in the shed between all the strands, with the thumb resting over the strands.

3. With the right hand, take strand 16 and pass it through the shed from left to right, as shown in Fig. 3. Strand 16 will now become strand 1 at the right.

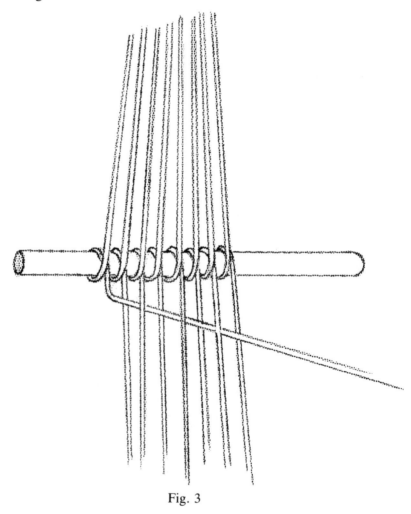

Fig. 3

4. Place the new strand 1 under the right forefinger. Insert the forefinger under the next strand (now 2), and over the next strand (now 3). Continue the

process, moving the right forefinger to the left, over and under the strands. When all are on the right hand, transfer the new shed to the left hand. Continue the process by passing the first left-hand strand through the shed. Repeat to within 7″ of the ends of the strands.

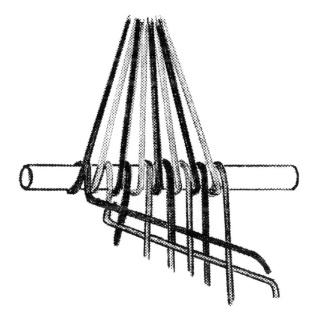

5. Gather strands 1 and 2 in the right hand and strands 3 and 4 in the left hand. Twist each pair of strands in the same direction by rolling them between the thumb and forefinger. Let the pair in the right hand twist with the pair in the left hand in the opposite direction, according to Fig. 4. Tie the end of the fringe and knot. Make three additional fringes by the same process and repeat at the other end of the belt.

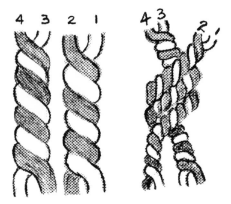

Fig. 4

PLAINS LINK BELT

Materials

cowhide strip or strap leather, 2″ wide by
   approximately 36″ long (length will depend
   upon the wearer's waist measurement)
2 leather thongs, each approximately 48″ long
sharp knife
awl or other pointed tool
ruler
pencil
leather-carving kit (steel stamping tool, swivel
   knife, pointed beveler) (optional)
permanent color markers (optional)

1. Measure waist and cut as many squares as neces-
   sary (a 24″ waist will require eleven 2″ squares).
   (Fig. 1.)

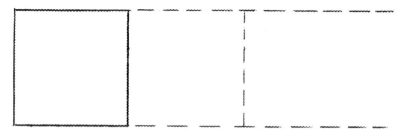

Fig. 1

2. With an awl or other pointed tool, punch holes, as shown in Fig. 2.

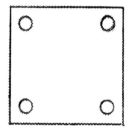
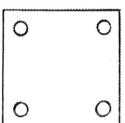

Fig. 2

3. If you wish, you can now draw a design on each square and color the designs with permanent color markers, or you can carve a design on each square. (Follow the instructions on the carving tool kit.)

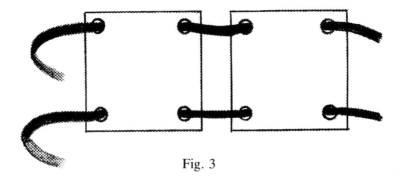

Fig. 3

4. Pull each of the two leather thongs through the holes in the squares, as shown in Fig. 3. Knot the four ends of the thongs, as shown in Fig. 4.

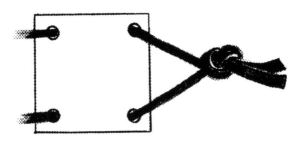

Fig. 4

15

Leggings, Breechcloths, and Aprons

Cloth or skin coverings for the legs were worn by Native Americans of both sexes. Men's leggings, most often worn with breechcloths, were loosely fitted. Some reached from the ankles to the crotch and were attached to belts; others were tied around the thigh. Women's leggings were more

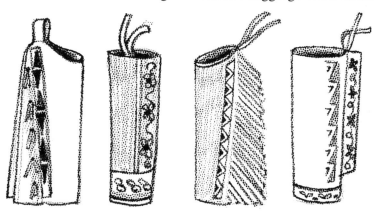

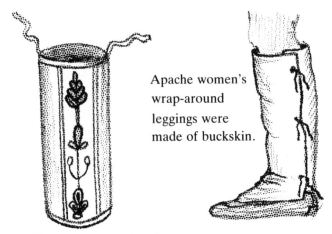

Apache women's wrap-around leggings were made of buckskin.

Ottawa women's leggings

close-fitting. They reached only to the knee, and were usually tied above the calf. In some tribes, such as the Apache, Ute, and Arapaho, women's leggings were fastened to moccasins to form boots.

The leggings of the California, Southwest, Plains, and Plateau Indians were usually fringed down the seam and at the bottom. Lakes, Southeast, and Northeast tribes wore leggings with front seams, which they often decorated with quillwork or beadwork. People in the Pacific Northwest had finger-woven leggings, made of the hair of the mountain goat and shredded cedar bark, and decorated with symbolic designs.

breechcloth

A breechcloth was simply a strip of buckskin or woven fabric, approximately one foot wide and six feet long. It was passed between the legs and under the front and rear part of a belt. Square aprons were sometimes substituted for breechcloths.

Sauk apron

Women also wore aprons. Generally made of dark cloth or of buckskin, they were decorated to match the wearers' moccasins and leggings.

PLAINS LEGGINGS

The following instructions and diagrams show how to make one man's legging. Repeat each step to make a pair. By following the instructions, you can make a pair of women's leggings, but they should be more closely fitted and extend only to the knee. Both men's and women's leggings can be decorated with beadwork instead of fringe (see Fig. 4).

Materials
buckskin, felt, or synthetic leather
tape or narrow leather strips (for ties)
pair of scissors
glover's needle and heavy-duty thread
paper or cloth for pattern
pencil
tape measure

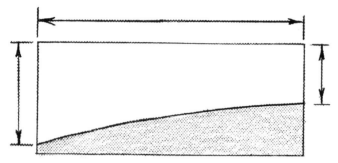

Fig. 1

1. Measure the circumference of your thigh and the length of your leg from mid-thigh to ankle. Cut a pattern according to your measurements and the outline shown in Fig. 1. Make sure you have enough room at the ankle for your foot to slip through. Allow 2½″ for the fringe along the seam of the legging.

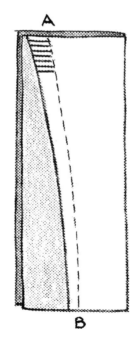

A

Fig. 2

B

2. Fold the buckskin or other material in half, lengthwise, pin your pattern to the material, and cut out
   the legging shape. Sew from point A to point B.
   Fringe the material extending from the seam, as
   shown in Fig. 2.

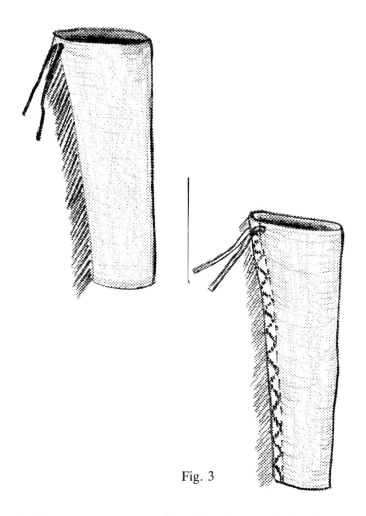

Fig. 3

3. Sew two tapes or strips of leather to the legging, as
   shown in Fig. 3.

16

Moccasins

Moccasins were worn by every Native American, with the exception of a few tribes in the Southwest and along the Pacific coast who preferred sandals or went barefoot.

Extremely comfortable and practical, this footwear was the first item of North American Indian apparel adopted by white explorers and settlers. Like the Indians, they found moccasins to be unequaled for woodland and canoe travel. And like the Indians, also, they often added long fringes to the heels of their moccasins in order to erase their tracks when on the warpath or while hunting game.

There were two traditional kinds of moccasins: soft-sole, with buckskin bottoms and uppers; and hard-sole, with rawhide bottoms and buckskin uppers. Each type was usually decorated with quillwork, beadwork, dyes, paint, or fur.

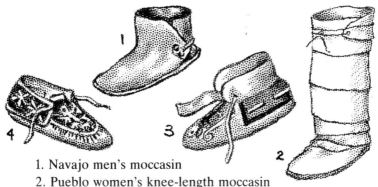

1. Navajo men's moccasin
2. Pueblo women's knee-length moccasin
3. Blackfoot painted moccasin
4. Chippewa beaded and quilled moccasin

The cut of the moccasin and its decoration identified the tribe to which it belonged. The footwear of the Chippewa, for example, reflected the meaning of the tribe's name: "people of the puckered moccasin." Apache moccasins had knee-high legs and turned-up toes that protected the wearers from cactus thorns and poisonous reptiles. The hard-sole moccasins of the sub-arctic, Paiute, Ute, and Navajo were made by molding wet rawhide around pieces of wood, shaped like feet. When the rawhide dried and the wood was removed, the leather kept its shape. Beaded buckskin uppers were then attached to the soles. Winter moccasins of the Lakes, Northeast, and Prairie Indians were made of buffalo or bear pelts, worn with the fur on the inside.

For authentic Native American moccasin construction, see the stitches shown in the chapter on skinwork.

Buckskin spats were often worn
over moccasins by both men and women.

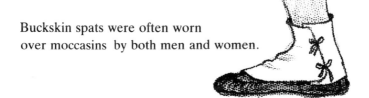

CHIPPEWA MOCCASINS

Materials
cowhide or synthetic leather*
leather thongs
shears
heavy-duty thread and glover's needle
sharp knife
tape measure
pencil
string (optional)
beadwork or quillwork equipment (optional)

*Felt may be substituted for other materials if the moccasins are to be worn indoors only.

Note: One pattern will fit both the right and the left foot. Repeat each of the following steps to make a pair. If you wish to decorate the moccasins with quillwork or beadwork, this should be done *prior* to step 5. (See chapters on beadwork and on quillwork.)

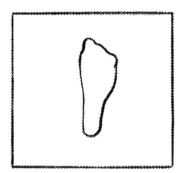

Fig. 1

1. Place your foot on the material and draw an outline around it, as shown in Fig. 1.

2. Measure and mark 2″ from the toe and each side of the ball of the foot (the widest part). Draw a circle around the upper part of your foot to points A, as shown in Fig. 2. Measure and mark an additional 2″ from points A to points B, and straight down to points C.

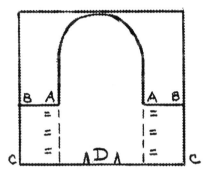

Piece E

Fig. 2

3. Cut into the material by clipping ¾″ from the bottom and 1¼″ apart at the back of the heel, point D, as shown in Fig. 2.

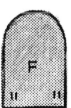

Fig. 3

4. With a tape measure or a string, measure around the entire ball of your foot. Stand on the string or tape and bring it up around your foot. Cut another half circle, F, one-third the width of the ball of your foot and one-half the length of piece E, from the toe end to points A, according to Fig. 3.

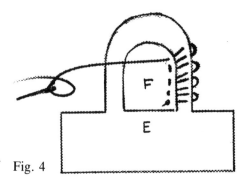

Fig. 4

5. Sew together pieces F and E, as shown in Fig. 4.

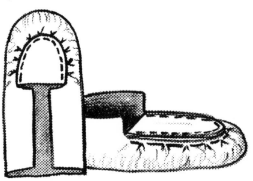

Fig. 5

6. Because the distance around piece E is almost twice that of piece F, piece E must be puckered at ½" intervals. To do this correctly, take a stitch through piece E twice the length of the corresponding stitch in piece F. Piece E will pucker and will have the same number of stitches as piece F. Pull the stitching tight, so that piece E puckers up over the side of your foot to form the toe of the moccasin, as shown in Fig. 5.

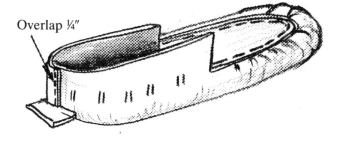

Overlap ¼″

7. Cut slits, G (shown in Fig. 2), in the widest part of the moccasin. These will be used for thongs and the moccasin tie.

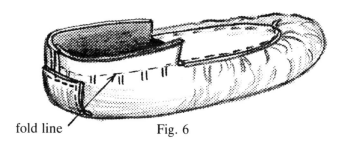

fold line   Fig. 6

8. Sew the heel, according to Fig. 6. Insert a thong through the slits, G, and tie. Fold down section I (shown in Fig. 2) to form a narrow cuff.

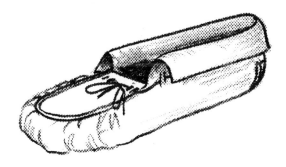

KIOWA MOCCASINS

Materials

cowhide or synthetic leather*
leather thongs
shears
heavy-duty thread and glover's needle
sharp knife
tape measure
ruler
pencil
string (optional)

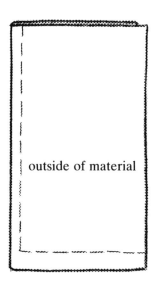

outside of material

Fig. 1 |

*Felt may be substituted for other materials if the moccasins are to be worn indoors only.

Note: While these moccasins are easy to make, you may wish to first make a pattern out of muslin or a piece of old cloth, such as an old sheet. This pattern is for the right foot. Reverse it for the left foot.

1. Fold the material lengthwise, as shown in Fig. 1. Measure and mark a line ½" from the fold and 1" from the bottom of the material. Place your foot along this line, as shown in Fig. 2, and draw a curve ½" from the top of your big toe and ½" from the ball of your foot. Continue to draw the curved line from the ball of your foot to the bottom of the material.

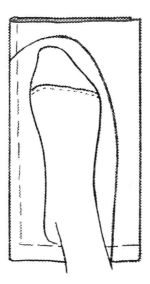

Fig. 2

2. Unfold the material and place it on a flat surface, as shown in Fig. 3. Place your foot on the center of the left fold, ¾" in from the bottom. Draw a curved line around your heel. Mark the place where your instep is, approximately at point A in Fig. 3. This will designate the place where the moccasin's tongue will be.

3. Draw a 2" line between points B and C. Then draw a line from the center of the points to the heel, point D. Cut along this line.

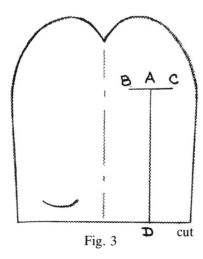

Fig. 3

4. Fold the material inside-out, so that the penciled lines are on the inside. Sew the material together around the toe and down to the heel, according to Fig. 4.

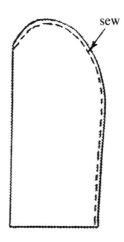

Fig. 4

5. Turn the material right-side out and cut the line, E—F, as shown in Fig. 5. If you place your right foot inside, while cutting, you will know precisely how far to cut.

6. Cut the line across the instep.

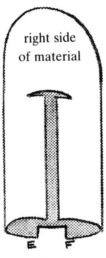

right side
of material

E   F

Fig. 5

7. Stitch the heel on the outside, according to Fig. 6. Sew the back of the heel, from the bottom toward the ankle. Then sew the back of the heel to the bottom of the moccasin.

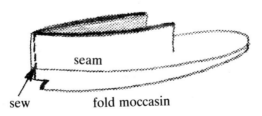

seam

sew   fold moccasin

Fig. 6

99

8. The moccasin should now look like the drawing in Fig. 6. Cut a piece of material for the tongue, 2″ x 3″, as shown in Fig. 7. Sew the 2″ side of the tongue to the moccasin.

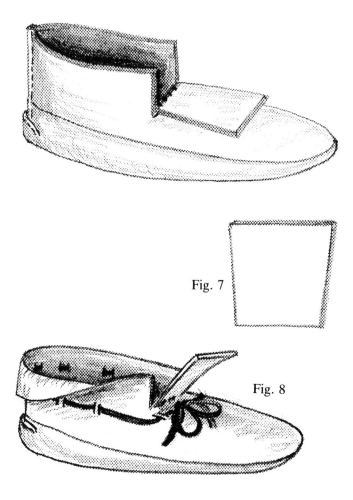

Fig. 7

Fig. 8

9. Cut slits at 2″ intervals, just under the upper flap, and pull a thong through them. The thong should be tied under the tongue, according to Fig. 8. If you wish, you can fringe the tongue.

17

Bags and Pouches

Since the Indians had no pockets in their clothing, carrying cases were essential adjuncts to the wardrobes of both men and women. Their bags and pouches were usually tucked

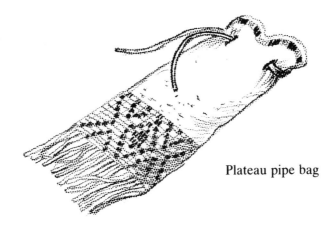

Plateau pipe bag

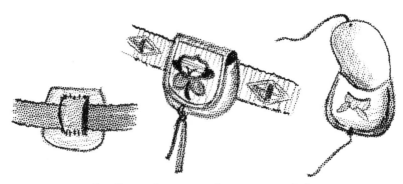

Small pouches were often worn on belts.

under or over belts, or attached to them by thongs.

Small pouches were used for carrying personal articles—paint, tobacco, medicine, and other prized possessions. Larger bags contained miscellaneous articles, such as sewing tools, pipes, dried food, and fire-making equipment.

The *parfleche,* or carrying case of the Plains Indians, was a rectangular envelope made of rawhide and decorated with painted designs. The Nez Percé, Ottawa, and other tribes of the Plateau-Basin region often wove bags out of cornhusks and deerskin strips, while many Lakes and Prairie tribes had carrying cases woven of moose and buffalo hair, mixed with nettle, milkweed, or hemp fibers.

Winnebago bags, woven out of twisted cornhusks and buffalo hair.

The majority of Indian carrying cases, however, were fashioned of soft buckskin or similar leather. They were sewn together with animal hair, grass, or *babiche* (thongs cut from deerskin or the skins of eels) and decorated with painted designs, beadwork, or quillwork.

SAUK CARRYING CASE

Materials

16″ x 24″ piece of light tan chamois, suede cloth,
   napped buckskin cloth, or felt
nylon thread
needle
pair of scissors
awl
pencil
ruler
colored felt-tipped markers (red, black, and
   brown)
acrylic paint and brush (optional)
beading needle and beads (optional)
leather thong, 24″ long

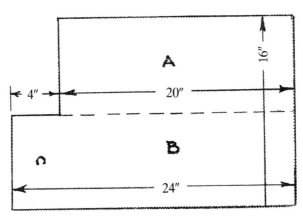

Fig. 1

1. Place material on a flat surface. Mark and cut
    according to the dimensions shown in Fig. 1.

103

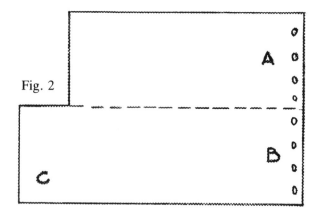

Fig. 2

2. With an awl or other pointed tool, make holes large enough to accommodate thong, ½″ from the top of A and B, as shown in Fig. 2.

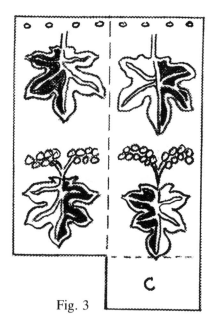

Fig. 3

3. With a pencil, draw designs on A and B, and color with felt-tipped markers, or decorate with paint or beadwork. (See chapter on beadwork.)

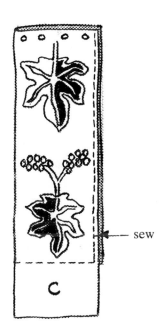

Fig. 4

4. Fold material and sew, as indicated in Fig. 4.

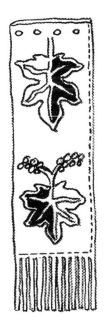

Fig. 5

5. Cut fringe on C, as shown in Fig. 5.

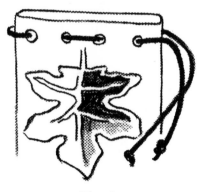

Fig. 6

6. Insert thong in holes, as shown in Fig. 6. Knot each
    end of the thong.

GROS VENTRE PARFLECHE

Materials

41″ x 22½″ piece of buckskin, napped buckskin
   cloth, or light-colored felt
3 leather thongs, each approximately 11″ long
1 leather thong, 20″ long
pair of scissors
awl
pencil
ruler
felt-tipped markers (assorted colors)
iron

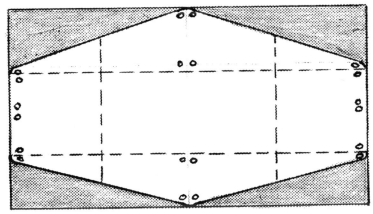

Fig. 1

1. With pencil, draw pattern on material, according to the dimensions in Fig. 1, and cut with scissors. Fold material, as indicated on dotted lines, and iron.

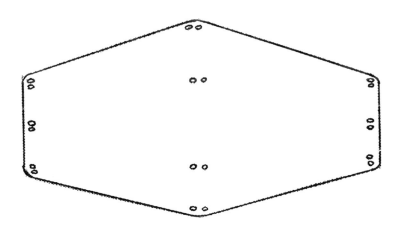

Fig. 2

2. With an awl or other pointed tool, punch holes for leather thongs in the material, as shown in Fig. 2.

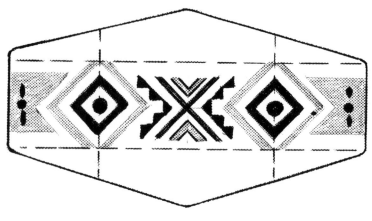

Fig. 3

3. With felt-tipped markers, paint designs on the outside of the parfleche, as shown in Fig. 3.

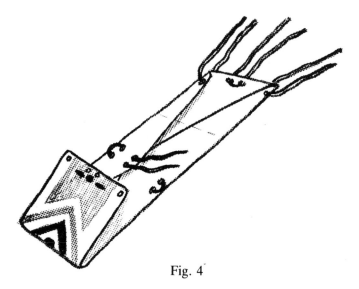

Fig. 4

4. Pull the thongs through the holes, as shown in Fig. 4.

Designs for decorating the parfleche

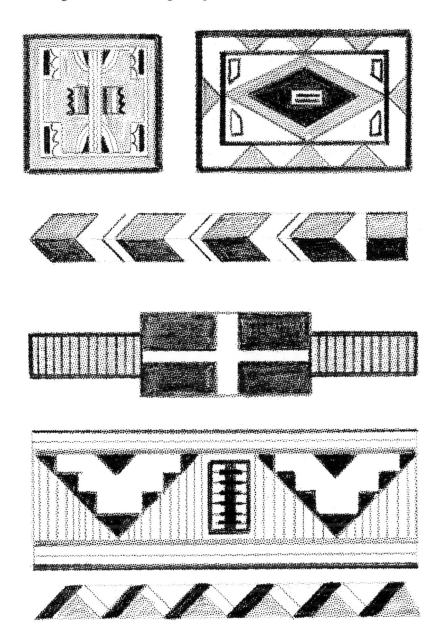

List of Suppliers

Crazy Crow Trading Post
107 North Fannin
Denison, Texas 75020

Grey Owl Indian Craft Manufacturing Company
150-02 Beaver Road
Jamaica, New York 11433

Plume Trading and Sales Company
Manufacturers of Indian Craft Supplies
P.O. Box 585
Monroe, New York 10950

Tandy Leather Company
3 Tandy Center
P.O. Box 2686
Fort Worth, Texas 76101

Western Trading Post
32 Broadway
Box 9070
Denver, Colorado 80209

Selected Bibliography

Curtis, Natalie. *The Indians' Book.* New York: Harper and Brothers, 1923. Republished by Dover Publications, Inc., 1968.

Hodge, Frederick W. *Handbook of American Indians North of Mexico.* New York: Rowman and Littlefield, Inc., 1965.

Hunt, W. Ben. *The Complete How-to Book of Indiancraft.* New York: Macmillan Publishing Company, 1973.

LaFarge, Oliver. *A Pictorial History of the American Indian.* New York: Crown Publishers, Inc., 1956.

LaFarge, Oliver. *The American Indian.* New York: Golden Press, 1960.

Parker, Arthur C. *The Indian How Book.* New York: George H. Doran Company, 1927.

Schneider, Richard C. *Crafts of the North American Indians.* New York: Van Nostrand Reinhold Company, 1972.

Tunis, Edwin. *Indians.* Cleveland: The World Publishing Company, 1959.

COMMON METRIC EQUIVALENTS AND CONVERSIONS

Approximate

1 inch	= 25 millimeters
1 foot	= 0.3 meter
1 yard	= 0.9 meter
1 square inch	= 6.5 square centimeters
1 square foot	= 0.09 square meter
1 square yard	= 0.8 square meter
1 millimeter	= 0.04 inch
1 meter	= 3.3 feet
1 meter	= 1.1 yards
1 square centimeter	= 0.16 square inch

Accurate to Parts Per Million

inches × 25.4	= millimeters
feet × 0.3048	= meters
yards × 0.9144	= meters
square inches × 6.4516	= square centimeters
square feet × 0.092903	= square meters
square yards × 0.836127	= square meters

Index

113